Life Cycle of an
Apple

Angela Royston

Heinemann Library
Des Plaines, Illinois

Published by Heinemann Library,
an imprint of Reed Educational & Professional Publishing,
1350 East Touhy Avenue, Suite 240 West
Des Plaines, IL 60018

Designed by Celia Floyd
Illustrations by Alan Fraser
Printed in Hong Kong / China

02 01 00 99
10 9 8 7 6 5 4 3 2 1

The Library of Congress has cataloged the hardcover version of this book as follows:

Library of Congress Cataloging-in-Publication Data

Royston, Angela.
    Life cycle of a apple / by Angela Royston.
        p.   cm.
    Includes bibliographical references and index.
    Summary: A simple introduction to the life cycle of a red delicious apple, from the blossoming of a flower bud in the spring through the development and ripening of the fruit to its harvesting in the fall.
    ISBN 1-57572-696-3 (lib. bdg.)
    1. Apple--Life cycles--Juvenile literature.   [1. Apples.]
    I. Title.
    SB363.R69   1998
    583'.73--dc21   98-10753
                                                       CIP
                                                        AC

Paperback ISBN 1-57572-472-3

Acknowledgments
The Publisher would like to thank the following for permission to reproduce photographs:
A–Z Botanical Collection/F. Merlet pp. 7, 8; Bruce Coleman/Christer Fredriksson p. 19; Harry Smith Collection p. 24; Holt Studios International/Inga Spence pp. 5, 18, Holt Studios International/Nigel Cattlin pp. 6, 13; NHPA/David Woodfall p. 11, NHPA/Stephen Dalton p. 12; Oxford Scientific/Terry Heathcote p. 4, Oxford Scientific/D.R. Specker p. 16, Oxford Scientific/Carson Baldwin Jr. pp. 20, 26-27; Roger Scruton pp. 9, 10, 14, 15, 17, 21, 22, 23, 25.

Cover photograph: Trevor Clifford/Trevor Clifford Photography.

Our thanks to Dr. John Feltwell, Wildlife Matters Consultancy, in the preparation of this edition.

Contents

What is an Apple?

An apple is a fruit that grows on a tree. There are thousands of different kinds of apple trees. These crab apples taste very **sour**.

late winter

early spring

I week later

The apples in this book are Red Delicious. They taste sweet and juicy. Every year each tree produces a new crop of apples.

spring

4 weeks later

summer

Apple Tree late winter

These apple trees are about ten years old. The trees have no leaves during the cold months of winter.

late winter

early spring

I week later

Each **twig** is covered with tight **buds.** As the days get warmer, the buds begin to open.

spring

4 weeks later

summer

Bud early spring

Inside the **bud** are tiny leaves. They push through the bud and grow bigger. Soon the whole tree is covered with leaves.

8

late winter   early spring   I week later

Leaves use water from the soil, sunlight, and air to make food for the tree. Pink buds are growing among the leaves.

spring

4 weeks later

summer

Blossom

The pink **buds** open out into small pinkish-white flowers called **blossoms**. Each flower has five petals with yellow **stamens** in the center.

late winter

early spring

I week later

Now the whole tree is covered with blossoms. The flowers smell sweet and the stamens are covered in a yellow dust called **pollen**.

spring

4 weeks later

summer

Pollination a few days later

This honeybee is flying from flower to flower. It collects **pollen** and stores it on sticky hairs on its back legs.

late winter   early spring   1 week later

Some of the pollen from one flower rubs off onto the center of the next flower. This pollen helps to make tiny apple seeds.

spring

4 weeks later

summer

The flower has done its job. The petals **wither** and fall off, leaving a tiny apple with the apple seeds inside.

14

late winter

early spring

1 week later

The apples begin to swell and grow.
The skin becomes waxy and shiny.
If you look closely, you can still see
the remains of the petals at one end.

spring

4 weeks later

summer

This is the caterpillar of a codling moth. It is just one of many insects that likes to eat the leaves and fruit of the apple trees.

late winter   early spring   I week later

A caterpillar has eaten a hole in this apple. Most farmers spray their trees to kill the insects before they damage the fruit.

spring

4 weeks later

summer

18

All summer the apples grow bigger and sweeter. These big red apples are now sweet and **ripe**.

late winter

early spring

1 week later

The whole tree is covered with juicy, red apples.

spring

4 weeks later

summer

Harvest early autumn

The apples are picked by hand
and stored carefully in big boxes.
If they are kept cool, they will last
all winter.

late winter   early spring   1 week later

Some of the apples fall to the ground before they are picked. Wasps and birds feed on the sweet **flesh** and the apples slowly rot.

spring

4 weeks later

summer

The apple trees are getting ready for winter. The leaves turn red and fall to the ground. As they rot, they slowly become part of the soil.

late winter

early spring

I week later

Buds have formed on the **twigs**. They will stay like this until next spring when they will open up into new leaves.

spring

4 weeks later

summer

24

Farmers **prune** the trees every winter. They cut off some of the branches to make the tree stronger.

late winter   early spring   1 week later

Inside each apple there are brown seeds. If they are planted, they might grow into new apple trees next spring.

spring

4 weeks later

summer

An Apple Orchard

This **orchard** produces thousands of **ripe** apples each year. Some will be sold to shops and markets. The rest will be made into pies or juice.

Apple trees start to grow fruit at three to five years. Most farmers usually replace their trees before they are twenty years old.

Life Cycle

Apple Tree

1

Bud

2

Blossom

3

Pollination

4

Growing

5

Harvest

6

29

Fact File

People have been eating apples for over 2 million years.

Apple trees only produce good fruit in places that have a cold winter.

We can eat apples all year round, because some countries have their autumn when we have our spring.

One apple tree may produce about 200 apples each year.

In an orchard apple trees may live for up to 100 years.

Glossary

blossoms a mass of flowers on a
  fruit tree

bud a swelling on a stem that will
  grow into leaves or a flower

flesh the juicy part of a fruit

orchard a field or garden where
  fruit trees are grown

pollen the tiny male seeds of
  a plant

prune to cut back a tree or plant
  to make it stronger and healthier

ripe fully grown and ready to eat

sour having an acid taste

stamens the parts of a flower
  that produce male seeds

twig a thin branch

wither to dry up and die

More Books to Read

Dowden, Anne. *From Flower to Fruit*. New York: Ticknor & Fields Books for Young. 1994. An older reader can help you with this book.

Maestro, Betsy. *How Do Apples Grow?* New York: HarperCollins. 1992.

Micucci, Charles. *The Life & Times of the Apple*. New York: Orchard Books. 1992.

Index